Ornamental Woodcarving

in the Norwegian Tradition

By
Johan Amrud

Heart Prairie Press
Whitewater, Wisconsin

This is the Third Edition. It has been revised, enlarged, and translated into the English language.

Editions One and Two, published in 1983 and 1985, are Norwegian Language Editions and were published by Universitetsforlaget in Norway.

This Edition was translated by Else Bigton and edited by Phillip Odden and Bob Mischka.

Printed in the United States of America

Heart Prairie Press
P. O. Box 332
Whitewater, Wisconsin 53190

Library of Congress Cataloging-in-Publication Data
Amrud, Johan.
     Ornamental woodcarving in the Norwegian tradition /
Johan Amrud.
     p. cm.
     ISBN 0-9622663-9-6

     1. Wood-carving--Norway. I. Title
NK9760.A47 1992   736.4'09481
                                  QB192-1122

Table of Contents

Foreword

In the past many people have asked me how they might be introduced to the woodcarving trade. Others have asked about the availability of my drawings. Many have asked if this type of information could be printed in a book.

It looked like there was a demand for this. Since the Universitetsforlaget also showed some interest, I decided to try it.

This book will show some of the programs used at the Hjerleid (Woodcarving) School in Dovre. The presentation will be an introduction to woodcarving and an illustration of some of the drawings I have worked out and used while teaching at the School. I show many pieces done by the students by which they have gotten their education, and which they have used for their journeyman's examination. I also have included a short history in the beginning of the book.

It is hard to give a full description of the training needed to become a woodcarver in a book. You cannot learn design by reading — you have to experience it through the process, and in the pieces themselves. The artist Trygve M. Davidsen says it this way: *"Learn to draw — learn to see!"* The same can be said about designing your work.

The required practice pieces are pictured, along with a short description. I do not show much of the technical side of woodcarving. There are books and pamphlets in print directed to the beginner woodcarver.

I would like to thank Jacob Sagflaten for his photography help. Thanks also goes to Ole Rønning Johannesen for his help with proofreading the art history, and to Sigurd Muri for proofreading and the layout of the Second Edition.

The last sections of this book are devoted to the woodcarving designs I have developed over the years. Patterns for these designs may be purchased from me or from Vesterheim, the Norwegian-American Museum in Decorah, Iowa. For more information on the purchase of patterns please see page 104. My designs are influenced by old handiwork and folk art traditions, and are developed from personal experience and design.

Many of the projects were developed to meet the students own wishes and interests. I would like to say thank you to all the students I had in training from the years 1958 to 1980 who shared my experiences in the School and who have helped to bring our traditions forward to the future.

Johan Amrud

The Origins of Ornamental Woodcarving

Egyptian

Decorative arts go far back in antiquity, and follow the human race through all of it's history. The Egyptians had a highly developed culture as early as 4,000 years before the Christian era. They decorated their everyday articles and buildings with ornaments and figure reliefs. Often the patterns were taken from nature, such as the papyrus plant and the lotus flower. Animal feet were used as decorations on table and chair legs. Egyptians worshiped the sun as God, using it as a motif and as a origin of their ornamentation.

Papyrus and lotus flowers

The Nile River was (and is) an important traffic artery for the Egyptians, making the boat an important means of transportation.

Grecian

Style and fashions change with the times, and often come back again and again. Hellenistic art is said to have had its influence on all later art. This antiquity art developed in Greece around the year 1000 B.C. and has been cultivated ever since. Many of its motifs and patterns are still used today — such as the Palmett (Palm Crown) used on cemetery monuments. Borders like meander and eggstar are also frequently used today. The acanthus leaf was used as a motif on the Corinthian temple pillar — on the upper portion called the *capital*.

The Dorian and Ionic capitals have simpler forms, but the Corinthian capital is considered the most beautiful.

A Palm Crown (Palmett)

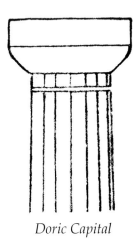

Doric Capital

Ionic Capital

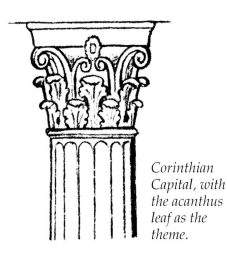

Corinthian Capital, with the acanthus leaf as the theme.

Meander Border

Running Dog Border

Egstarr Border

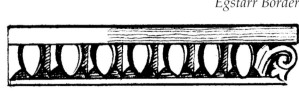

Nordic Iron Age & Viking Period

Old Christian art and the Nordic Iron Age meet in Norway in the prehistoric and saga ages, and create a magic style and form. In Norway we have many rich monuments from the Viking era. Many farms were cleared and settled during this period.

Blacksmith Art

Woodcarving has exerted an influence on a wide variety of things in Norway — from small decorative objects to furniture and church art. Many preserved gravemarkers are beautifully carved, as are the portals on our stave churches. Some churches are filled with rich, beautiful woodcarvings. In our museums we can study this special hand-work, a part of our best folk art. The most famous of these museums is Maihaugen with its exceptional collections from Gudbrandsdalen, and the Norsk Folk Museum in Bygdøy with collections from town and country. Our forefathers had great creative abilities and a strong pride in their work.

"Genuine everything should be, a mark the thing should have. A reminder of its author, a witness to him in all its days. Even on a harness pin they put their mark when it was done well. The tools were so-so, and many times lacking. Poor was often what they had. Even so the work was satisfactorily done." (Olav Aukrust)

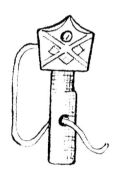

Harness Pin

A Bumerker is a mark used as a signature. These are found on the wall in the Fåvang church. Every farm had their own mark which they put on tools and household goods. It is probably connected to the old runic writing from prehistoric times. These marks would also protect the home from sorcery and injury to both people and animals.

The well known ship finds from Oseberg and Gokstad in Vestfold and from Tune in Østfold are witness to the exceptional woodcarving art done during this period, dating from about 800 A.D.

The grave dig at Oseberg was done by archaelogists in 1904. The masters who did this carving had had a rare imagination and creative power which we can only admire and accept today. We seem unable to reach this level of excellence in woodcarving today.

The Oseberg ship is not only a witness to the wood-carver's art. The boat has a fantastically fine and well shaped form which corresponds with it's function.

The Viking ships can be seen at Bygdøy. The *Kings Saga* tells us that Olav the Holy carved a dragon head on one of his ships. At that time the Kings had great pride in being good craftsmen. It was during thise period that the dragon style was developed and had its greatest influence.

Handle on a Viking sword at the Historic Museum.

Ormen Lange was the name of the long serpent on Olav Tryvasan's largest and best ship. The gold-leafed head would shine in the sun.

A beautiful coat of arms done during the viking age

Detail on a sword handle from a grave in Vest Agder

A distinctive ornament from about 400 A.D.

Styles of Ornamental Woodcarving

Dragon Style

The stave churches in Norway, with their distinct dragon style, coincide with the Romanesque style period in the early part of the middle ages. There were about 1,300 stave churches built during this period, with most in the 12th Century. Only thirty-two are left today. A distinctive development within the dragon style has been given the name "Urnes Style", from the Urnes stave church in Sogn. This has been recognized as the high point of this style. But there are so many masterpieces in the dragon style, both in composition and execution, that it is hard to call one the best.

The names of the masters who produced this fabulous woodcarving art are little known, and have been forgotten. However, their monuments are still standing and they tell, in their own quiet and marvelous language, about the times gone by. The Dragon style is said to be the most native woodcarving art in Norway.

The portal from Urnes stave church in Indre Sogn

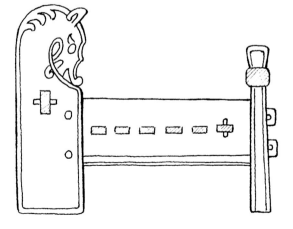

Romanesque Style

The style most common in Europe from the 900s to the 1100s A.D. is the Romanesque style — also called the architectural style. It developed individual characteristics in different countries. The Romanesque style began with the Roman Catholic Church. The Romans made use of the round arches in their architecture. The important architecture in the Romanesque style include the transept in the Nidaros Cathedral and nave in the Stavanger Cathedral. It has massive bearing walls with small openings for windows. Door openings and windows also have arches.

As mentioned before, many stave churches were built in Norway in the 1100 to 1200s, and many patterns were developed in this period. They still used some plant forms as motifs, but they were very stylized. In the lifelike ornamentation they braided in animals and fable animals. On the stave churches we can see a mixture of many of these motifs.

Baptismal Font

Romanesque Ornamentation

A vaulted style of door opening. The design on the arch was often repeated on other ornamentation.

Gothic

Around 1200 A.D. the Romanesque style was succeeded by the Gothic style. In Italy it did not develop fully but in Northern and Western Europe the Gothic was prominant until it was pushed aside by the Renaissance.

The Gothic style originated in France. The pointed arch was now used instead of the round arch, with lots of artistic engineering. It has dense planes and openings between the construction elements. The style is *sky-reaching*. The pointed arch is also repeated in the door and window openings. The chancel in the Nidaros Cathedral has both Romanesque and Gothic styles.

In this period the sculptures were free, loose, and finely draped. The ornamentation was mostly leaves with the grapevine and oak leaves used as motifs. Geometric patterns were also used.

In Norway the Gothic had very little influence on the woodcraft of the early middle ages.

Detail of a chest ornamentation done in the Gothic Style

Example of Gothic ornamentation on a bed from South Germany, done about 1500 A.D.

Sketch showing the pointed arch in the Gothic style

Renaissance

The Gothic period ruled from 1200 A.D. through the middle ages. The Renaissance style which replaced the Gothic originated in Italy in 1400 to 1500 A.D. Renaissance means revival or renewal of the Antiquity.

They had many motifs to build from. They wanted clean lines and harmony. An ornamental element called the *cartouche* was much used. It had a simple form and often had a nameplate in the middle. Flower urns and animal skulls were common motifs in the Renaissance, with realistic vines and acanthus leaves coming from them. Cherubs could also be mixed into the pattern.

Frames and mouldings were much used (and are a sign of the style). In Norway the Renaissance coincided with the depression after the Black Death, and also with the reformation in 1537. This made this style less prevalent in Norway than in most other countries. For example, the large, exterior church decorations were not used — new simpler fixtures were made and put in their place. Pulpits from this time have flat, simple ornaments. The early Renaissance made greatest use of the acanthus motif in it's ornamentation.

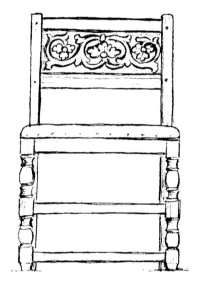

A Renaissance chair

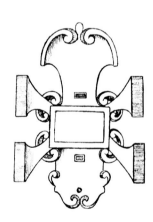

Cartouche ornament with nameplate in middle

A Renaissance ornament with a goat skull and flower urn

Baroque

Our art history tells us that the Baroque style also originated in Italy. It started in the middle 1500s and developed from the Renaissance style. The Baroque style was
powerful and expressive with strong, grand movements.

Baroque ornament was rich and vigorous with the acanthus plant as its main motif. It wound and formed itself
in many beautiful and splendid variations. The acanthus
is a thistle-like plant that grows in the Mediterranean
countries, often growing along the roadsides.

The Hellene (Greek) people were the first to use this
plant in their ornamentation. Later it spread all over the
world. From Greece to Gudbrandsdal as Roar Hauglid
writes in his books titled *Acanthus*. Blooming Baroque
(or acanthus baroque as it is also called) had a lasting
influence on our folk art (and Norwegian National art)
around the 1700s, especially in Gudbrandsdal. The acanthus motif was used in many different ways and variations. It was transformed and almost made a separate
style of its own in Norway.

In Gudbrandsdalen the style is called both krullskurd
and Dølaskurd "scroll carving".

In Telemark, Hallingdal, and parts of Norway's west
coast we find that rosemaling was the more common
form of folk art, even though there was much woodcarving done there as well. A well known woodcarver at that
time was Lars Kinsarvik.

*Simple acanthus designs
in the Baroque style*

Mirror design in the Baroque style

A Boroque armchair.

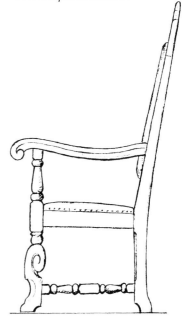

Rococo

Rococo is the name of a style developed in the early 1700s. It originated in France and is considered a feminine style. It is said that Madame Pompadour in Ludwig the Fifteenth's court helped create the Rococo style. She was the most powerful woman in the country at that time. The style is light, lively and a little wild in its composition, with many variations. The ornament is asymetric, often it incorporating a "C" shape. In this style there are many forms, including shells, mussels, palm branches, acanthus leaves and flowers. In Norway this style was more conservative. One variation, called peasant Rococo, had a heavier and stiffer form.

Rococo did not get as wide a reception as the acanthus motif among the woodcarvers around the country. It was much used among the rosemalers, especially in Hallingdal and Telemark. The violin got its clean and final form during the Rococo period. The Hardanger fiddle, however, had many interesting and fine forms before the Rococo form came along.

The styles that came after Rococo are of little interest to the woodcarver since they put less importance on the ornamentation. The most appropriate and common styles for woodcarving are Dragon, Renaissance, Baroque, and Rococo.

After Rococo the foreign influences on folk art diminished. There are many books to choose from for anyone who wishes for more detailed instruction of the different styles. One such book is *Stil og Smak i 6000 år*, by C. Hopstock and St. Tschudi Madsen in 1967. Another is a pamphlet of Ole Rønning Johannesen, *Stilhistorie*, Fabritius, 1970, — a simple and well illustrated booklet that would be good for use in schools.

Design for a Rococo armchair. Note the difference between the Baroque and Rococo chairs.

A Rococo style element

*Rococo design
from an old stove*

A typical Rococo ornament

Gudbrandsdalen Masters

Jacob Klukstad (1700-1773)

Many well-known woodcarvers in Gudbrandsdal have done many good pieces of art in the 1700s, in churches, homes, and on the larger farms. On the exterior of buildings and in the courtyards you would find signs of the woodcarver as part of the entrance, the carved gable ends, and the beautiful vehicles and church sleds. Some of the farms are now protected and stand today as they did then — in their beautiful and harmonic form with a good structure that fits nature and the valley milieu.

Front side of pulpit in the Skjåk church with gilded carving by Klukstad

Jacob Bersveinsson Klukstad is considered the most important master woodcarver of this period. He put his mark on Gudbrandsdal scroll carving. Klukstad was born in Nyrnesodden. After marrying he lived a while in Bøverdal, on a place called Runningen. He later moved to Lesja and settled in Klukstad under the parsonage. On his gravestone, beside the church, it is written he was born in 1705. His most famous work was done in the Lesja church about 1749. Later he worked in the Skjåk, the Heidel church, and others.

It has been claimed that he had no education and that he was untrained in the woodcarving trade. If his work in the Lesja church was one of his first, as claimed, then he was born a master. (Personally I believe he had both study and practice behind him before he was hired for this work — his biggest masterpiece.)

Ivar Kleiven writes this about him: *"The greatest master of all the woodcarvers in the Lom settlement was Jacob Bersveinsson Klukstad. His best work is so good that you have to search for them if anyone can do it better."* I have to agree with this, especially when it comes to composition and the overall effect — it is masterly done! He had an inate creative ability and a sense for beauty of form.

Harry Fett states: *"Klukstad can be counted as the creator of the typical Gudbrandsdal acanthus school-the scroll carving. He transformed the city's acanthus and gave it its own rich life."*

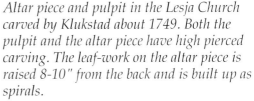

Altar piece and pulpit in the Lesja Church carved by Klukstad about 1749. Both the pulpit and the altar piece have high pierced carving. The leaf-work on the altar piece is raised 8-10" from the back and is built up as spirals.

Østen (Eistein) Guttormssøn Kjørn (1727-1805)

Among the other big masters in the north valley was Østen (Eistein) Guttormssøn Kjørn from Vågå. He later moved to Heidal. He did carvings in the Kvikne and the Sel church. The carvings in Kvikne church are copies of Klukstad's carvings in Heidal. Klukstad did not like this *"Because Kjørn stole his art."* Kjørn's carving is more stiff and not as lively as those of Klukstad, but he accomplished large and beautiful pieces over a wide area. Østen Kjørn was also a poet. I have seen a little handwritten book by him which also included some psalms.

The altar piece and pulpit at the Kvikne church, done by Østen Kjørn. In the altar piece a little bit of green color is added.

Sylfest Skrinde (1731-1785)

Sylfest Nilssen Skrinde was from Skjåk. He was Klukstad's journeyman, and did part of the work on the Heidal Church. His carvings are fairly flat — mostly acanthus leaves with a touch of rococo.

Interior of the Andersstua. The cupboard is made by Sylfest Nilssen Skrinde and shows a little of his distinctive style

Skjåk Ola (1744-1802)

Skjåk Ola, also called by the name "Teigroen", was a typical cabinetmaker and he has left many monuments. He had exceptional creative ability and fantasy. The motifs for his carvings are varied — especially well composed and formed in his own way. The execution could be better, especially on the cabinetmaking; but the whole piece is masterful. Some of his cabinets are kept at the Kunstindusti museum and at the Folke museum. A part of his carving has a touch of rococo in the composition of the patterns and drawing. A different type of cabinet made by him can be seen at the Maihaugen Museum.

A Skjåk Ola cupboard.
Shown in Andersstua on
Bjørnstad. Maihaugen.

Jacob Sæterdalen (1754-1821)

Jakop Sæterdalen was from Lom, but moved to Vågå. He carved a pulpit with a vaulted ceiling in Lom's old stave church. He had his own cupboard type of carving called Sæterdalsskåpet. There are many of these left. One of them is at Maihaugen where we also find cupboards by Skrinde. Sæterdalen's carving is similar to that of Klukstad, but flatter and simpler. He was an unusual character and there are many stories about him.

Detail of pulpit in Lom Stave Church with gilded carving by Jakop Sæterdalen

Sæterdalen's cupboard

Bjørn Olstad (1705-1764)
Johannes Segalstad (1711-1772)

Two of the most well-known woodcarvers, and the first acanthus carvers in the south Gudbransdal valley at this time, were Bjørn Bjørnsen Olstad, Øyer and Johannes Ellingsen Segalstad from Gausdal. They were church carvers. Segalstad also worked outside of the valley. The carvings of these two masters are somewhat coarser and more divided than that which Klukstad carved. The carvings were similar to those which the trademarks master Lars Pinnnerud did at Furnes.

Olstad carved the pulpit with a domed ceiling, kings monogram, and lions in Øyer Church. He also carved the fixtures in the Tretten Church. (I restored the lions in Øyer a few years ago.) Johannes Segalstad carved the pulpit in East Gausdal Church and Fåberg Church. A mangleboard from Segalstad with his special style is to be seen at Norsk Folke Museum.

The pulpit in Øyer Church by Bjørn Olstad

Korskille with lions in Øyer Church by Bjørn Olstad

*Altar in Skjåj Church carved
by Jacob Klukstad*

Kristen Listad (1726-1802)

Kristen Listad, originally from Sør-Fron, lived for a while at Segalstad on a farm which lays on the backside of Fåvang in Ringebu.He was characterized by Harry Fett as being the "Flower master from Ringebu." Listad is considered, along with Klukstad, as one of the greatest and most distinctive masters in the valley. He carved the lions in the korskillet in Fåvang church, the domed ceiling, and the crucifix. He also did some work in Sødorp church.

The korskillet in Fåvang Church has an expressive and beautiful form with the king's monogram from that time in the middle. The lions have the acanthus vine as foot hold and base, and are masterfully crafted with a rare bearing and power.

Listad carved churches and also smaller things. He left many beautiful and valuable pieces at different places — also outside the valley. In soapstone he also left his distinctive mark.

(Editor's Note: A korskillet is the area behind the altar where the choir stood.)

Korskille in Fåvang church by Kristen Listad.

Lars Pinnerud (1700 to 1762)

Lars Pinnerud from Furnes is well renowned. He also went up to Dovre and carved the pulpit with domed ceiling.

Per Haugen (1892-1961)

Per Haugen from Vågå carved the new Skåbu church in the late 1920s. He used Klukstad's style, but with his own personal clean and sensitive form. One would dare say he cultivated the style. The carving in the church is all finished with an oil stain and careful color tones so that the wood grain shows through. The decorative painter Davidsen from Oslo was entrusted this work.

Per Haugen also worked well in soapstone. He carved many beautiful grave markers that are standing in many different cemetaries around the valley. In his later years, he was master carver at the Hjerleids Husflidskole in Dovre.

Detail of pulpit in Dovre Church by Lars Pinnerud.

Pulpit in Skåbu Church by Per Haugen.

Mathias Fjerdingren (1901-1980)
Edvard Bakkum (1916-1975)

Mathias Fjerdigren was the master at Heidal Church after it was rebuilt after the lightening fire in the 1930's. His carvings are copies of the originals done by Klukstad. He and his helpers also carved in the Kvam Church after it was rebuilt after the fire in the war in 1940.

Fjerdingren worked a little in soapstone in later days. He did, among other things, the baptismal font in Dovrefjell and a few grave markers.

Edward Bakkum was the master carver doing the figures at both Heidal and Kvam.

Alterpiece in Kvan Church carved by Mathias Fjerdingren (acanthus) and Edvard Bakkum (figures).

Lars Prestmoen, Sør-Fron (1871-1957)

In the publication Kunst og Kultur (Art and Culture), 1959, Sverre Hov gives us a little insight into Lars Prestmoen and his woodcarving art. Prestmoen was a quiet and shy artist — probably less well-known than some others because he didn't do large pieces. But what he created is beautiful and perfect in form, giving both happiness and pleasure to the viewer.

He started as a shepherd-boy, as many did at that time in the valleys. In that way he learned to know and love nature. Hov tells further that it was Dr. Holst who discovered his gift when he was young, and had him sent to Dovre when Christiania Kunstindustrimuseum (Christiania – Oslo– Art Industry Museum) had started a craft school. It was said that Lars often walked between Fron and Dovre (about 48 miles each way) and carrying food on his sled, during that winter.

Shepherd boy, carved in wood, by Lars Prestmoen.

The principal at Dovre was Hans Lindsø — Lars' first teacher. The style Lars learned he called "The Dovre Style". In Lillehammer he met a good woodcarver named Odde. From him Lars learned a new style "Vågåstilen".

Prestmoen put in his biggest efforts with G. Larsen from Lillehammer (Pipe-Larsen). There he carved his most detailed and finest work on the Larsen pipe. His work was well known, both in Norway and in other countries. His wish was to carve a church, but this wish did not come true.

Lars Prestmoen carved many models for silversmiths, including the Prillar-Guri needle, the Birkebeiner needle, and the famous ram-motif. Not many people know who created these fine silver needles, which women have used to adorn themselves at many festive occasions. One of Prestmoens pieces, called Gjetargut – Shepherds Boy (taken from the publication), shows some of his talent and his imagination. Lars Prestmoen died in 1957 – he was 86 years old.

Gravestones by Different Masters

*Marker by Per Haugen at
Skåbu Church*

Marker by Vågå Church

*Gravemarker done in wood by
Iver Hølmo at Vågå*

Marker by Johannes Myrom, Vågå

Marker by Edvard Bakkum at Vågå

For additional information on acanthus carving the reader is encouraged to consult the book *Acanthus*, by Roar Hauglids.

Soapstone marker in Ringebu by Per Haugen

Marker by Sel Church by
Mathias Fjerdingren, Heidal

"Let us not forget our forefathers. They gave us our inheritance to follow, and it is more important than we can imagine." **(Ivar Aasen)**

Professional Training in Norway Today

Establishment of Hjerleid Program

By a King's resolution of September 10, 1948 a program was established for the teaching of woodcarving. The full training for this trade is now set for three years. Hjerleid vidaregåande school in Dovre was approved by the department in 1973. It is the only school in Norway today giving complete skills in woodcarving.

As mentioned in my Introduction, this book shows many of the drawings I have developed for the Dovre students to pass their journeyman's examination at the end of their apprenticeship. Students from all over Norway have since completed their apprenticeship since 1973. Their final pieces were judged by the Olso municipal committee for woodcarving.

To pass the journeymans examination by this plan you have to be skilled in three different styles of woodcarving, both in drawing and in carving, and must be able to carve in many different types of wood.

Besides the practical training the program includes drawing, stylistics, and the general theoretical subjects included in the apprentice law.

Practice Pieces in Different Styles

Chip Carving

Flat Carving

Acanthus

Dragon Style

Renaissance

Rococo Sytle

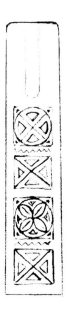

Mangle boards can also be used as practice projects

Simple Projects for Beginners

Chip Carving

Norwegian woodcarving can be divided into three types: chip carving, flat carving, and high carving. It is easiest to start with a simple chip carving pattern (chip carving is international). You can use a piece of pine the size of the drawing. This project can be done with just two tools, the V tool and a skew. Use the V tool for the coutours and the skew for the deeper cuts.

Combinations of these chip carved squares can be combined into a mangle-board. You can also get good practice in forming by making a handle for the board. Here the knife will come to its rightful place as the old and well-known tool that it is. The handle is most often formed as a horse.

Chip carving can be traced back to the middle-ages. The patterns are usually geometric, making simple but decorative designs that can be used on many things.

*Extending the pattern
for a mangle board*

A typical chip carving design

Flat Carving

The second type of carving is called Flat Carving. In Gudbrandldalen it is also called lesjaskurd. As a rule it has a shallow bottom and is without any forming or rounding of the pattern.

The Renaissance style has somthing in common with the flat carving with its simple and stylised plant ornaments.

This form of carving is often used on stabburs and door posts in Telemark and Setesdal. You will also find it on smaller interior woodwork.

Flat carving is a good second project with its simple form and flat-bottoming. In this project it is necessary to use different types of tools, including gouges and bottoming tools. After finishing these projects you can extend the pattern for more practice, gaining more understanding of techniques and materials before moving on to the next project.

Mangle board carved in the flat carving style

More Flat Carving Designs

An example of extending the pattern

Acanthus Carving

As the third project we can start with the well-known acanthus motif. It seems to maintain its popularity, even into our own time, for ornamentation.

These projects build further on what one has learned earlier about carving down and bottoming. One can also use a router to take some of the bottom out, making the work go faster and easier.

What is new on these first projects is the modeling or forming of the high relief (high carving) with the different leaves. Having an example of a finished, carved piece next to you while you work so that you can study it and compare is a big help. As a rule it is necessary to do many studies and projects in order to learn this type of carving, and to get to know the acanthus ornament. Having a drawing, with shading, is also helpful during this part of the training.

The first forming of the Acanthus Ornament.

More Acanthus Designs

*Mangle boards carved in the
Acanthus Style.*

Pierced Carving

Until now the carving projects all have had a bottom. Now we will take this bottom out, and will have what is called a pierced carving. A pierced carving often has a more lively form than one which is not pierced. A drill or jigsaw can be used to remove some the stock on a pierced carving. Back carving is an important part of pierced carving.

In the altar and pulpit carvings the pierced carving came into its full glory. (Note that Klukstads carvings have back carving that make the leaves thinner and lighter.)

Plate Shelf with a pierced acanthus design

Designs and Projects

Relief and Figure Carvings

Dragon Style Carvings

The Dragon style has low relief and often little model-ing, somewhat similar to flat carving.

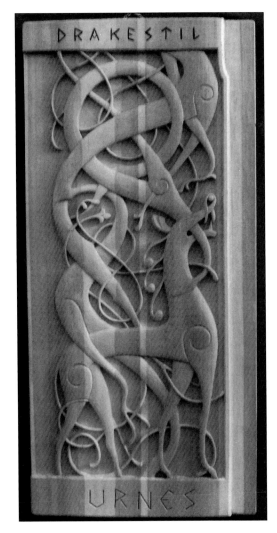

Renaissance Style Carvings

The pictures show two different Renaissance ornaments. Some Renaissance ornaments are close to Baroque. These designs are carved in oak.

Rococo Style Carvings

Top of mirror frame.

Mirror frame.

Clock frame.

Baroque Style Carvings

A "Bosskast" was used to keep hair brushes and combs. It's usually placed between two doors, and often had a decorative towel hanging underneath.

Pine bench with cushions.

Buffet cabinet with acanthus carved panels

*A copy of a type of hutch done by Sjåk Ola. The original is at the
Kunstindustry Museum in Oslo. This is the top section only.*

The Stabbur was an important building on the farm. Food and many valuable things were kept there. The door had to have a good lock and solid straps, made by the local blacksmith artist.

Student Bjørn Sørvang (left) with the author and some of Bjorn's pine and birch figure carvings.

Journeyman exam carvings by Svein Tore Kleppan in 1974, the first class from the Hjerleid School.

Scenes at the Hjerleid School

Additional Designs for which Patterns are Available

Mirror Frames

Full-size patterns for the carvings pictured in the balance of the book can be purchased from the author or from Vesterheim, the Norwegian-American Museum in Decorah, Iowa. For details see the information at the end of the book.

Pattern #40

Rococo mirror frame carved in birch. The background is painted blue and the foreground is covered in gold leaf. Pattern #72.

Mirror Frames (continued)

Mirror design in the Baroque style
Design #93

Mirror frame
Pattern #37

Wall Clocks

Wall Clock, Pattern #14

Clock case, Pattern #28

Wall Clocks (Continued)

Wall Clock, Pattern #19

Bentwood Boxes

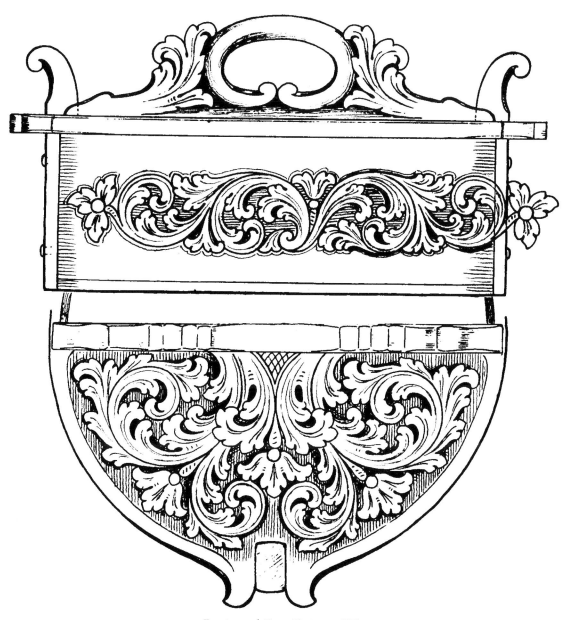

Bentwood Box, Pattern #31

Bentwood Boxes (Continued)

Bentwood Box, Pattern #46A

Grandfather Clocks

Grandfather Clock, Pattern #55

Grandfather Clocks (Continued)

Grandfather Clock, Pattern #54

Detail of door design.

Stein

Small Stein, Pattern #45

Bellows

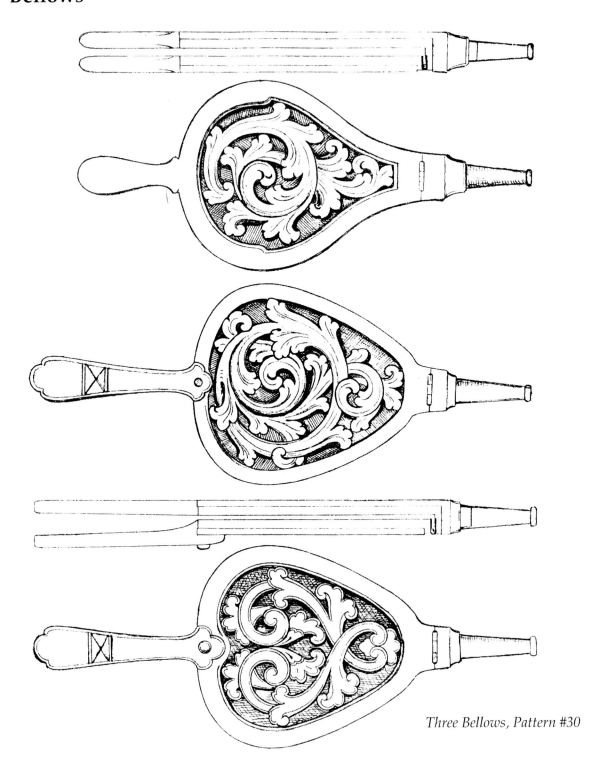

Three Bellows, Pattern #30

Bellows (Continued)

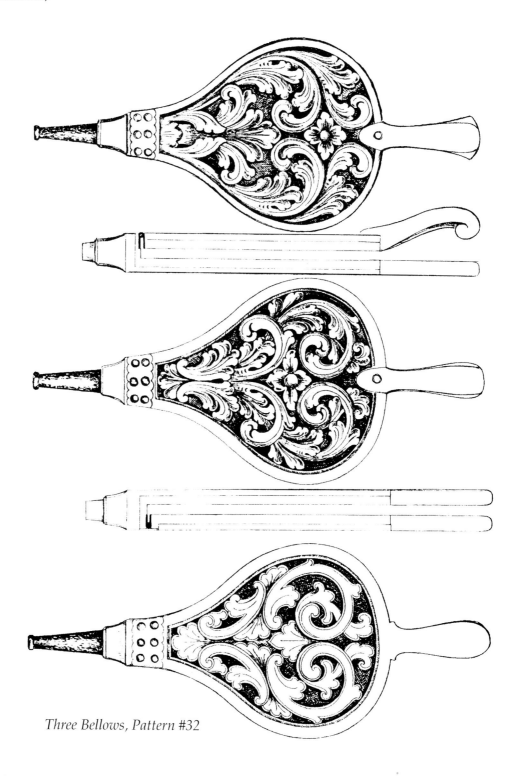

Three Bellows, Pattern #32

Spoons

Spoon, Pattern #42

Spoons (Continued)

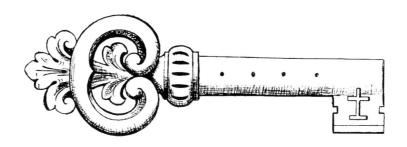

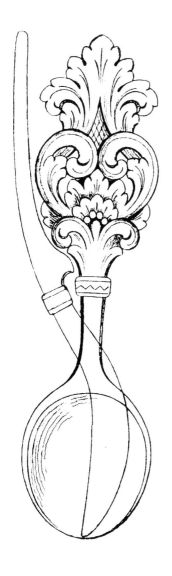
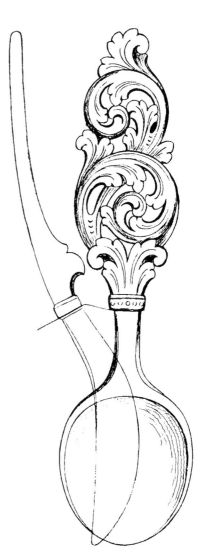

Key and two spoons
Pattern #90

Spoons (Continued)

Two spoons, Pattern #82

Lamps

Two-armed Lamp, Pattern #80

Lamps (Continued)

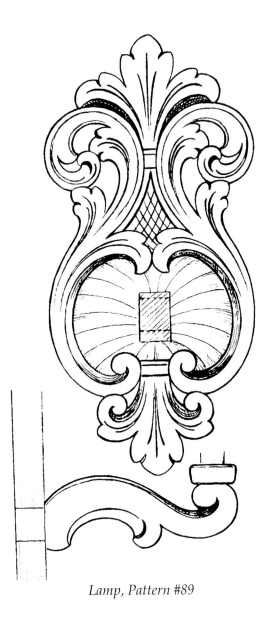

Lamp, Pattern #89

Lamp, Pattern #87

Lamps (Continued)

Two-armed Lamp, Pattern #85

Lamps (Continued)

Lamp, Pattern #83

Mangleboards

Two Mangleboards, Pattern #34

Mangleboards (Continued)

Two Mangleboards, Pattern #38

Mangleboards (Continued)

Two Mangleboards, Pattern #39

Cradles

Cradle, Pattern #46

Cradle, Pattern #24

Cradle, Pattern #46

Plate Shelves

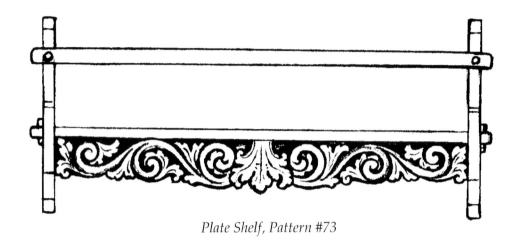

Plate Shelf, Pattern #73

Plate Shelf, Pattern #73A

Wall Cabinets

Corner Cabinet, Pattern #18

Wall Cabinets (Continued)

Wall Cabinet, Pattern #29

In addition to the wall cabinets depicted in this section, the pattern for the Bosskast shown on page 45 is also available. It is pattern #67

Wall Cabinet, Pattern #27

Wall Cabinets (Continued)

Wall Cabinet with Plate Shelf
Pattern #75

Medicine Cabinet, Pattern #60

Corner Hutches

Corner Hutch
Pattern #5

*Corner Hutch
Pattern #7*

Hutches

Small Hutch, Pattern #76

Copy of hutch originally done by Skjåk Ola, and shown on page 20
Pattern #9

Hutches (Continued)

Large Hutch
Pattern #10

Details of Hutch #10

The hutch belonged with the built-in furniture on
the farm. The craftsmen travelled around the
country and made each piece at the location
where it would go. The livingroom hutch was
often so big it would not fit through the door.

Construction details of Hutch #10

The top section of Hutch #10

Sliding door panels for Hutch #10

Chairs

Armchair, Pattern #91

Chair, Pattern #11

*The design on this chair is
complimentary to the design
for the sofa on page 98,
Pattern # 12.*

Chairs (Continued)

Baroque Armchair (King's Chair)
Pattern #71

Rococo Chair made of birch
Pattern #70

Miscellaneous

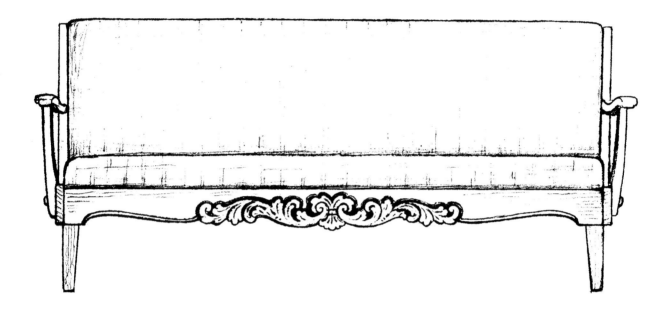

Sofa, Pattern #12

The design on this sofa is complimentary to the design for the chair pictured on page 95, pattern #11.

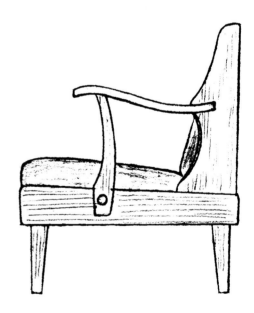

The Senge Benk (Bed Bench) pictured in the background on page 53 (top picture) is also available, as Pattern #65. This is a very functional piece of furniture, with a storage compartment under the hinged seat. In the old days the compartment under the seat would be used in the evening as a child's bed.

Porridge Bucket, Pattern #35

Miscellaneous (Continued)

Buffet with relief carvings, Pattern #23

Trestle Table, Pattern #21

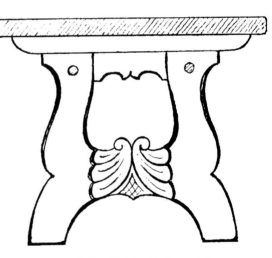

Coffee Table, Pattern #41

Small Box
Pattern #86

A travelling case was a small trunk used by men when going to town. It was reinforced with iron straps and had handles on the sides — well done and grand. Often they were both carved and painted. On this one we have put legs under it and converted it into a sewing box.

Travelling Case made into a Sewing Box
Pattern #36

*Trunk
Pattern #56*

*Trunk
Pattern #77*

*Secretary
Pattern #8*

The patterns on the preceeding pages have been drawn by the author, and are protected by copyright. Copies of these patterns can be purchased from either the author, in Norway, or from the Vesterheim museum in Decorah, Iowa. The patterns are full sized, and include construction details as well as the carving designs.

Purchasers of the patterns, or of this book, are prohibited by copyright law from making copies of these patterns to sell or to give away. It is also prohibited for a person to use these patterns in a trade or business, for the purpose of making a profit, without first making the proper arrangements with the author.

To purchase patterns please contact either of the following to get a copy of the current price list:

> Johan Amrud
> 2634 Fåvang
> Norway
> Phone (062) 84 534
>
>   or
>
> Vesterheim Norwegian-American Museum
> 502 W. Water St.
> Decorah, Iowa 52101
> Phone (319) 382 9681

Weaving on a loom decorated with acanthus designs.